ADAM Plus One

Teresa Joyelle Krager
Illustrated by Joezie Mitchell

ELK LAKE PUBLISHING INC
PUBLISHING THE POSITIVE
Plymouth, Massachusetts

Cover and Interior Design: Joezie Mitchell, Derinda Babcock

Editor(s): Derinda Babcock, Deb Haggerty

Illustrations: Joezie Mitchell

PUBLISHED BY: Elk Lake Publishing, Inc., 35 Dogwood Drive, Plymouth, MA 02360, 2021

Library Cataloging Data

Names: Krager, Teresa Joyelle (Teresa Joyelle Krager.)

Adam Plus One / Teresa Joyelle Krager.

32 p. 21.6 cm × 21.6 cm (8. 5 in. × 8. 5 in.)

Identifiers: ISBN-13: 978-1-64949-306-4 (paperback) | 978-1-64949-307-1 (trade hardcover) | 978-1-64949-308-8 (trade paperback) | 978-1-64949-309-5 (e-book)

Key Words: Christian children's books, Adam and Eve, children's Bible story, children ages 4 to 8, Christian rhyming picture books, children's Jesus Book; children's inspirational

Author Dedication

To Bruce, my husband and partner

Illustrator Dedication

To Val—

Because of you, I learned I could
do hard things.
I pray someday, I can inspire others
like you have me.

My name is Adam,

And I think you should know

In the Garden of Eden

A looooong time ago,

One thing was "not good."

God said so. It's true.

Let's look back. I'll explain

The what, where, how, and who.

2

Before time began

Earth was empty and dark

Until God spoke the word

And light burst—a great spark!

Beams broke through the darkness.

God called the light "day."

(He knew that His children

Would need light to play.)

4

God stretched wide the sky

And spread shores for the seas.

He laid out the land

Adding plants and tall trees.

A sun for the day,

Moon and stars for the night,

Fish, birds, and land creatures

"Good" in God's sight.

6

Then from the dust
Of the ground, God made man.
He breathed into me
And my new life began.

An image of God,
I could love, laugh, and climb.
I could think, I could speak—
Just for fun—all in rhyme.

8

Then God said, "Not good,"
Because I was alone.
I needed a partner
With skin and with bone.

God gave me a job,
A new garden to tend,
But would I find a helper,
One like a true friend?

God brought me the birds

To give them a name.

I spied fliers and swimmers,

Some wild, others tame.

But birds weren't real friends,

Even though some could talk.

I could *not* share a nest

With an eagle or hawk.

12

So …

I focused on fish.

I might give them a name,

But in most every way,

Man and fish weren't the same.

The fish lived in water,

While I breathed the air.

We could *not* live together,

Could *not* be a pair.

14

God sent the land creatures.
I named every kind,
But were *any* like me
With my language and mind?

I looked all around
With a little frustration.
God listened and smiled
At each brief explanation.

Frogs were too slimy,
Bears—too hairy,
Pigs—too muddy,
Crocodiles—scary!

16

Turtles—too slow,
Sloths—too sleepy,
Apes—too silly,
Centipedes—creepy!

17

Giraffes were too tall.

And mice were too small.

18

The cat and the dog
Were my favorite of all.

Yip!

Peep!

Purr...

20

From aardvarks to zebras,

I called them by name.

Each creature unique,

From Creator's hand came.

But none equaled man,

Not with yip, purr, or peep.

We needed one more …

So God sang me to sleep.

22

Then He took out a rib,

Closed the skin in that place,

Formed a woman named Eve,

And we met face to face.

The same but yet different,

A beautiful sight.

Adam plus woman,

Partners just right.

24

God finished creating
When 'Adam plus none,'
A looooong time ago,
Became 'Adam plus one.'

God said, "Rule the earth,"
For together we could.
God saw all He made
And He said, "VERY GOOD!"

About the Author

Teresa J. Krager,
With a master's in education,
Taught twenty-seven years,
K and first grade dedication.
With Seuss in her head
And a Spirit of inspiration,
Points others to Jesus,
God's Son, our salvation.

Teresa lives with her husband
In a desert location.
Five kids and five grandkids
Bring much celebration.
Loving music, songwriting,
And a mountain vacation,
She's thrilled to highlight
God's awesome creation in
Adam Plus One

www.teresakrager.com
www.pointingtheway.live

Also by this author: *Before Your Birth Day*

About the Illustrator

Joezie Mitchell has loved drawing since she was old enough to hold a pencil. She lives with her family in the beautiful Pacific Northwest, and when she's not drawing, she enjoys competitive swimming and spending time with her sweet dog Calvin (he's her favorite of all). *Adam Plus One* is Joezie's first published picture book.

CPSIA information can be obtained
at www.ICGtesting.com
Printed in the USA
LVHW070112220522
719421LV00004B/13

* 9 7 8 1 6 4 9 4 9 3 0 7 1 *